DITTY BOX

It's a funny old life!

*A Selection of Poems and Songs
in a Light-hearted Mood*

DAVID LEGGETT

with illustrations by

Andre Ellis & **Jenny Stevens**

Rollston Press

Ditty Box
By David Leggett

ISBN-13: 978-1-7326121-6-7
ISBN-10: 1-7326121-6-1

Front cover and typesetting by Serpentine Design, Cadgwith, Cornwall, UK

Back cover painting by Jen Stevens

ROLLSTON PRESS
1717 Ala Wai Blvd, Suite 1703
Honolulu, Hawaii 96815
USA
www.rollstonpress.com
info@rollstonpress.com

Introduction

My dictionary defines *ditty* as 'a short simple song or poem'. *Ditty Boxes* were small, strongly-constructed wooden chests with locks and brass nameplates, issued by the Royal Navy to sailors and marines in the period 1870-1938. Inside these, men would keep their treasures, private papers and photographs. The example illustrated on the front cover was my Father's – issued to him in 1915.

The words of all the songs and poems laid out in this little collection are original and written by me. I do hope that you enjoy them! They were written spontaneously when the muse happened to be upon me, from the late 1990s until the present day. They include themes based on everyday life experiences, my own quirky take on 'the human condition' and subjects that some amongst us might find to be amusing (or irksome!). Some were written to celebrate individual occasions.

Most of the short offerings come under my heading of 'Occasional Verse'. Before being styled 'Verse' in retirement, some of these served working time as e-mails!

The music for the songs has been arranged simply, in 'easy' keys and adapted (mostly) by me from a variety of sources. I have tried to credit those sources when I've known, but some have obstinately refused to give up their authorship, so if I have trodden on anyone's toes or copyright in some small way, I apologise.

My lyrics are free from any restriction for amateur use but before any commercial reproduction or publication, please ask me.

David Leggett, April 2019.

Acknowledgements

I claim credit for just one tune here: my eccentric and naive little 'Gurnard Waltz'. The version included is one kindly transcribed for duet concertina by Pauline Wallace.

I know that Andre Ellis' drawings scattered among the texts and scores will add enormously to the appeal of this little volume. Thanks also to Jen Stevens and William Blake for use of their watercolour vignettes.

I am grateful to Robin Bates, who has encouraged my efforts over the years and has guided my inept hand in all things musical. Any musical errors existing herein are however, mine alone!

Design and print realisation is by Bill and Jake Scolding.

CONTENTS

Poems and Songs

Occasional Verse

Tune

IT'S A FUNNY OLD LIFE!

D.L.

Unknown

Oh, you're born, and you die,
Not knowing the how or the why,
You can't understand though you try.
It's a funny old life!

The meaning of life is obscure,
What's the present, the past, the future?
Sometimes it is hard to endure.
It's a funny old life!

Though you may think this quite weird,
It seems time and matter appeared,
In a 'big bang' and now the smoke's cleared,
It's a funny old life!

Oh! The stars in the sky,
Made the matter that makes you and I,
And uranium and apple pie.
It's a funny old life!

Is the universe a machine,
Shaped by merciless forces unseen?
Or can we see where God's hand's been?
It's a funny old life!

Declaim:
Where we are going to, no-one can tell,
Plump for oblivion, heaven or hell.
If you ask my opinion, I'll answer you: 'Well,
I just think it's a funny old life!'

THE CADGWITH COVE INN SONG

D.L.   Anon.

It's the Cadgwith Cove Inn for me,
Overlooking the wide restless sea:
It's friendly and bright, you get treated alright,
There's nowhere that I'd rather be!

People travel from near and from far,
For a drink in its quaint little bar.
If there's beer and it's nice, you can stomach the price,
So why not come down for a jar?

Mine Hosts are a jovial pair,
Greet you warmly whenever you're there.
It's always implicit they'll enhance your visit,
They're sociable, generous and fair.

If you're ever in need of a laugh,
Why not chat to the jolly bar staff?
They're honest and true and they won't diddle you
Out of anything more than 'a half'.

With the regulars you can relax,
They don't gossip, nor do they bite backs.
After having one drink with them, you'll swim or sink with them,
Of good-natured banter, there's stacks.

The food that you're served when you dine,
Is unequalled by any Rick Stein.
The landlord's the chef here, and he is quite clev-ere,
He makes a nice profit on wine!

Though this may seem too good to be true,
There's a warm welcome waiting for you.
There's music, there's singing... and the till keeps on ringing,
You could be part of it too!

*This song was written in 2002 when the pub was operating under
a different regime. The first verse may be used as a chorus, if desired.*

RAPUNZEL

D.L.

Trad

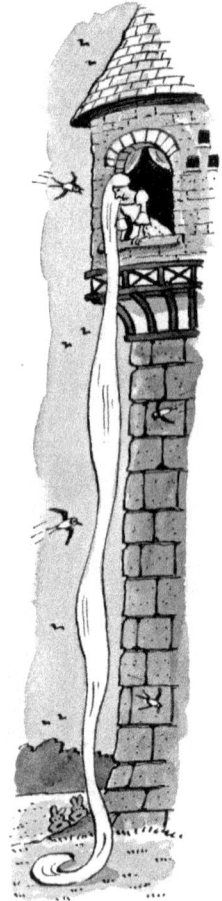

A wicked witch who with her e-vil power, Confined Ra punz - zel in a loft-y tower.

The tow-er had nei-ther lad-der nor stair To asc-end was to climb her long blonde hair.

A wicked witch, who with her evil power,
Confined Rapunzel in a lofty tower.
The tower had neither ladder nor stair,
To ascend was to climb her long blonde hair.

The witch would visit daily by this route,
And feed the beauty with exotic fruit.
The damsel thus atop the tower was bound,
And dearly wished her feet on solid ground.

She had resolved this plan a long time since,
To importune some handsome passing prince.
She'd plait her hair into a climbing rope,
And by this means, the couple would elope.

The day she'd waited for, it came along,
A wandering prince had heard her own sweet song.
She let down her hair as an invitation,
Though was dismayed by his prevarication.

'I've had adventures all my own young life,
'Tis time I settled down and took a wife.
Fain would I climb, to taste of your delights,
But sadly, never had a head for heights'.

SOCKS AND SANDALS

If only someone could release
Us from the dratted style-police!
Socks with my sandals I can't sport,
Without inviting cruel report.

Without the socks, my feet get burned,
By sun, or chafed (a lesson learned).
There is no reason I can find,
Why people should be that unkind.

Some fashion guru might explain,
Why it's so 'wrong' to wear the twain,
But where I cannot see the science,
I find no reason for compliance.

(In Japan, both young and hoary,
Wear the flip-flops they call 'zori'.
With these, 'tabi' socks they wear,
No-one there would think it queer!)

THE CADGWITH – RUAN MINOR CAR-REVERSING TANGO

D.L.

Unknown (Tango)

You'd think it would be sim-ple if you took a car and drove,

From Cadgwith up to Ru-an in a hur-ry from the Cove,

But hangon just a minute! There's nothing sim-ple in it,

The Cadg-with Ru-an Min-or Car-Re-ver-sing Tan-go.

You'd think it would be simple if you took a car and drove,
From Cadgwith up to Ruan in a hurry from the cove,
But hang on just a minute, there's nothing simple in it,
The Cadgwith – Ruan Minor car-reversing tango.

You're just up to pub corner and there's suddenly in view,
A great big green Range Rover and it's bearing down on you.
Someone's parked in the passing-place, leaving insufficient space,
Now you're doing that car-reversing tango.

You're just at Rene's cottage, and things are getting worse,
Great grandad in a Morris Minor, he can't find reverse:
Gears are crunching merrily, he'll be very glad to see,
You're doing that car-reversing tango!

You're just up to Tremarne now, quite near your journey's end,
But a flashy silver Mercedes, it comes around the bend.
If he's spent fifty thousand pounds, you'd think his driving would be sound,
That this time, he'd do that dratted tango!
He's got five yards to back-up, much too difficult for him,
So, you find yourself reversing back a hundred yards to Tim's:
He's very grateful, he knows it would be hateful,
For him to do that car-reversing tango!

The next time that I go to Ruan, I'll forget the car,
And stamp it breathless up the hill, it's easier by far.
Those non-reversing arses should take some dancing classes,
The Cadgwith – Ruan Minor car-reversing tango!!

OLE!

When sung, the phrases in italics are repeated.

THINGS THAT FLOAT IN ON THE TIDE

D.L.

Arftur Sullivan

Cornish wreckers of old were resourceful and bold,
As they surveyed the scene on the shore.
Useful jetsam and flotsam, they usually got some,
And often they went back for more.
Whether ships timbers fine or a hogshead of wine,
And much handsome booty beside.
Their lives were enriched, as on the beach pitched,
The things that float in on the tide.

We trust the Good Lord to provide,
By the things that float in on the tide.

Now for flotsam and jetsam, you go down to get some,
A bit after high waters hour.
A seagull takes a meal from the corpse of a seal,
As the tideline you carefully scour.
You slip down with a yelp on some rotting old kelp,
And other things you can't abide.
There's a mangled tree root and an old welly-boot,
With the things that float in on the tide.

The Good Lord may still yet provide,
By the things that float in on the tide.

There's some bright orange plastic, some knicker elastic,
A polythene bottle or two.
Someone's been inept with a used contraceptive,
There's gobbets of black tarry goo.
There's an aerosol can and a drowned Action Man,
Who lost his left leg when he died.
There's a crab's carapace and a limp cardboard case,
With the things that float in on the tide.

The Good Lord once used to provide,
By the things that float in on the tide.

THE TESTIMONIAL

D.L.

Trad. Scot. (Brochan Lom, Pt. A)

This testimonial I write to you this happy day,
Your product has transformed my life, I'm very pleased to say.
Of your company I have become the very greatest fan,
This letter is the grateful thanks of a contented man.

My life was as successful as good fortune could arrange,
When all-too-quickly came about the most unwelcomed change.
My health and wealth so suffered as result of this affair,
My wife and I became very demoralised pair.

In the Sunday paper I discovered your advertisement,
And to try a sample of your product, my small cheque I sent.
It came wrapped-up discretely in a brown paper package,
And I have to say I rate it as the wonder of the age!

I was so delighted that my lot be thus improved,
That to write to you this endorsement, I very quickly moved.
Please send to me a year's supply without further delay,
This testimonial I write to you this happy day.

Yours faithfully,

MY UNCLE BERT'S A VIKING

D.L.

Anon. Arr. Robin Bates

My uncle Bert's a Viking,
He sails the stormy seas.
With shipmates bold, in climates
        cold,
They do just as they please.
He ploughs the northern ocean,
For plunder and for lust,
And when he's had his wanton way,
You won't see him for dust.

Some day for a diversion,
He'll burn a monastery,
Or desecrate young virgins,
By way of revelry.
He wears a horny helmet,
A battle-axe and sword,
Strikes fear in the hearts of coastal
        folk,
Who tremble at his word.

Bert sails the North Sea over,
His bloody sword in hand,
From Reykjavik to Dover,
A scourge by sea or land.
His drunken raiding parties,
Lay waste to many a shore,
And though you think he's gone away,
He'll soon be back for more.

But when he's in his home port,
There's peaceful things to do.
Bert often bakes some fairy cakes,
And shares them with his crew.
He's quite a flower arranger,
And seldom known to curse,
And in his quieter moments,
He'll write some gentle verse.

I WAS DRACULA'S DENTIST

My day's work was done, the last patient gone,
When he entered my room quite unbid:
A ghoulish thin bloke in a red-lined black cloak,
With a flourish of which, in he slid.

He gave me a scare when he sat in the chair,
'A check-up' the frightening gent hissed.
I saw his dentition, realised my position,
For I'd become Dracula's dentist!

With no holly stake, or the courage to make
The world free of vampires, I fear.
I had to defer, and when finished with 'Sir',
I felt quite unsteady and queer.

His check-up complete, he got to his feet,
And I followed him out in the gloom.
No person I saw as I stood at that door,
But a bat's silhouette 'gainst the moon!

*A poem written for a Halloween recitation. I suppose it would seem too
frivolous if made into a song using the tune of 'I was Kaiser Bill's Batman' ?!*

JANE AUSTEN'S WORLD

A rhyme I'll tell to you, and set a scene,
Of country middle classes and their mien,
Where many a vacuous, idle lady strives
To make intrigue from uneventful lives.

Of minor landed-gentry, curates, bores,
Prince Regent's time, when women wore no drawers,
And dandies in knee-britches did indulge,
The better to display their manly bulge.

To cultivate their manners and attire,
Young ladies of this class, they did aspire.
The 'empire line' their bosom upward thrust,
The better that their chin might touch their bust.

Squalor and want scarce touched their precious lives.
Their fondest dream was love as rich men's wives
And heedless of the plight of rural poor,
These gentry rarely passed their humble door.

But we must now attend the Squire's ball!
A sumptuous feast's preparing in his hall.
To dance with Captain Fortescue is grand:
I'm hoping soon he'll ask me for my hand!

BARMAN'S BLUES

Workin' in a pub bar, fightin' to keep up.
Landlord says 'it's easy work', but I've been 'sold a pup'.
I've got to earn a livin': little else to choose.
There's poor consolation in them barman's blues.

Chorus
I got the blues, I got the blues, I got them awful barman's blues,
I got the bl-u-u-es *(yodel!!)* them awful barman's blues!

Punters three-deep at the bar, they entered in a rush,
And they all shout 'it's me next', they start to whine and push,
But I've got just one pair of hands, to serve them with their booze,
The odds are stacked against me and I know that I must lose.
Chorus

Two barrels, they need changin', and beer-pipes to wash through.
The ice pail's nearly empty, glass collectin' still to do.
Telephone is ringin', glass-washer's blown a fuse.
A hopeless situation gets you barman's blues!
Chorus

The manners of some customers are vexin' and they're rude,
You'd think the world was endin' when you tell them 'there's no food'.
They treat you like a cypher who will soak-up their abuse,
You get broad shoulders carryin' the barman's blues!
Chorus

'Tis sometimes asked why blue men really can't sing whites,
Without the accusation that they are hypo-crites.
I'll answer that another time when beer's not in my shoes,
Or I'm a person sufferin' the barman's blues.
Chorus

MY SECOND HOME

D.L.

after Glover-Kind (1907)

Oh! I'm on the commuter train each morning,
For to get to my work in the city,
And I work so very keenly, that my salary's unseemly,
And the pressure's always on, and my leisure time is gone,
But just for a week or two each summer,
I deserve to have a little luxury,
For I paid out hard-earned cash for it,
And eagerly I dash for it,
My second home in Cornwall by the sea!

Oh! I've got a very roomy off-road vehicle,
Just perfect for my family and me.
Back home we do the shopping, there's little point in stopping,
At the village store where it's a bore to buy your grocery.
Oh! There are a few eccentric friendly locals,
Relics of a one-time quaint community,
But no matter what their plight,
I will defend my right,
To my second home in Cornwall by the sea!

Oh! I've often thought that I might just retire there,
I'd be an asset on the local scene,
But I know that there's a doubt that I'd like what it's about,
It's lacking any culture and it's not so very clean,
And how would I cope without 'the theatre',
And sophisticated fellow-souls like me?
Though for fifty weeks it's void,
Why are you so annoyed,
By my second home in Cornwall by the sea?

IT AIN'T CRESS OR CELERY, SO

D.L.

It ain't cress or celery so,
It ain't cress or celery so.
Just ask your greengrocer,
He'll answer you 'No Sir,
It ain't cress or celery so.'

Globe artichoke's make lots of waste,
They cannot be eaten in haste.
Tomatoe's are fruity,
Aubergine's have their beauty,
But they haven't much of a taste.

Now if you're a jolly old Greek,
It's cheese in your salad you'll seek,
And what could be better
Than a few chunks of feta,
To get with your shoppin' next week.

Now onion's, they may make you weep,
But lettuce, it won't make you sleep.
When unable to slumber,
Try countin' cucumber,
Instead of the usual sheep.

It ain't cress or celery so,
It ain't cress or celery so.
When singin' a ballad,
Pertainin' to salad,
It AIN'T cress or celery, SO!

Please note: correct use of the 'greengrocer's apostrophe'?

REMEMBERED DREAM

Dav Id

♩ = 80

I dreamt that I had met a cat, That read a book to me. It turned the pages with its tongue whilst sitt - ing in a tree And then up - on a rhu - barb leaf I surfed a - cross a cor - al reef And land - ed on a palm-fringed isle set in an az - ure sea.

I dreamt that I had met a cat,
That read a book to me.
It turned the pages with its tongue,
Whilst sitting in a tree
And then upon a rhubarb leaf,
I surfed across a coral reef,
And landed on a palm-fringed isle,
Set in an azure sea.

A smoking volcano grumbled,
Above the island's trees.
The ground, it trembled and I stumbled,
Down upon my knees.
A naked dusky maiden ran
Toward me on that alien strand,
Tumbled beside me in the sand,
In a sulphurous breeze.

We rolled in passion on the ground,
She pinned me underneath.
I noticed then, perhaps too late,
Her rows of white, sharp teeth.
A lava flow was on its way;
I must withdraw without delay.
I woke up to a dawning day,
Back home, to my relief!

WINTER

When towering waves assail the coast
And sparrows huddle in their roost.
No visitors the Cove hath seen.
Over the road the tide hath been.
The fishing-boats, up from the beach
Are hauled, beyond the sea's wild reach.
As storm-clouds scud across the sky,
Some sportive gulls do bravely fly.

When brown foam off the sea doth blow
And bank accounts are ebbing low.
Cold rain doth beat against the door!
And snow hath lain up on the moor.
When on the hill the breath doth rasp
And Melancholy tests its grasp.
Of earthly comforts there's a dearth,
Then seek we solace of the hearth.

OCCASIONAL VERSE

When some of these weren't busy being verse, they were busy being e-mails

Taking the Pith?
The putative Mayor of Cadgwith,
Assembled his kin and his kith,
And some that stood with he,
Gave rhymes, (doubtless pithy),
Whilst others stood *taking* the pith.

Ocklynge
The worthies that live at Ocklynge,
Arranged a fine evening binge.
The setting, bucolic, though quite alcoholic,
Spouting limericks that made us cringe!

Midland Ladies
Three ladies of Midland-ish climes,
Were given to outlandish rhymes.
A surlier critic might have been less politic
About their poetical crimes.

Rubaiyat
In life one thing is certain, time will fly.
Behold! approach last Tuesday in July.
Then give Aladdin's lamp another rub,
To conjure music genie down in't pub!

Xanadu
Tomorrow night did Jen and Dave,
Astutely, 'barbecue!' decree,
Where 'alf a dozen of us plan,
To burn a sausage, crack a can,
Could Robin come for tea?

Avast!
Would you tonight a Pirate be?
(the Penzance pub, lad, NOT 'the sea'!)
There'll be no need for sword or pistol,
But you might wish to bring your whis-tle.
A carriage could be at your door,
At seven-thirty, not before.
If buccaneering is for you,
Just signal the Ashanti crew!

Dinner Invitation
This is no prolix,
This is no bolix,
If you are able,
To grace our table,
Friday's my offer,
Dinner to proffer.

Om Proper Suffolk
Matthew, Mark, Luke 'n' John,
Ho'd tha? dickey woil I gi? on,
I gen'r'lly talk a load a squi?,
But tha? don'? ma??er, no? one bi?!

? represents the East-Anglian glottal stop

Local Doxology
or 'Through Rose-Tinted Spectacles'
Prazegooth from whom all blessings
flow,
And likewise Cadgwith here below,
Let Grade and Ruan be our boast,
And to them all we'll drink a toast!

Might Invalidate Guarantee
If I had a washing machine,
I'd use it to keep my clothes clean,
Although I'm not fussy,
I wouldn't wash pussy,
Or false teeth,
D'y'know what I mean?

I misunderstood. Mary's false teeth did go accidentally into the washing machine, but the cat had climbed into the tumble drier. Fortunately it was soon noticed and stopped before major injury could happen.

Oh! Oh! Marconi-o
Oh! Oh! Marconi-o,
He came this way,
Brought his materials,
Set up his aerials,
Sent his wireless telegraph,
To ships far out at sea,
Locked up Dr Crippen
With a Morse Code key.

Haiku
Grey fingers of cloud
Are interlacing in front
Of an orange moon.

THE GURNARD WALTZ

Transcribed for duet concertina by Pauline Wallace

♩ = 120

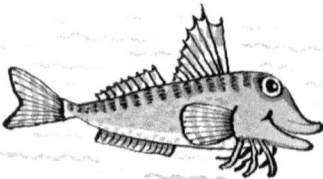
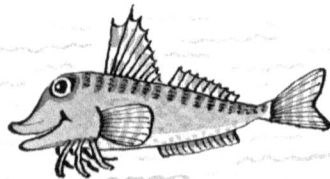

David, 1950

David Leggett

David spent the earlier years of adult working life as a chemist in manufacturing industry.

His fortieth birthday became a catalyst for dramatic change, joining in a partnership to operate a successful freehouse pub in Cornwall. Further changes led to him running a small hotel and relief-managing a variety of Cornish pubs.

Later, adapting what had been a lifelong passion – metalwork – into a means of support, he designed and made silver jewellery for over twenty years.

David has always been at heart an indigenous musician (he plays concertina) and 'wordsmith'. This little offering is his first venture into publishing.

David lives with his partner Jenny on the Lizard Peninsula in Cornwall.

www.ingramcontent.com/pod-product-compliance
Lightning Source LLC
Chambersburg PA
CBHW071801020426
42331CB00008B/2359